# Hope: Brightest Cruel Of Life

## A Tale of The Void Fueled by Hope

Amogh Jha

India | USA | UK

# Dedication

To the people who are stuck in the **Void** of their **Own
Creation.**
To **Life** for being the best **Muse.**
To the part of me who loves creating.

# Preface

A book with few poems describing how **Hope is a Fuel** which keeps us alive but at the same time burns us, along with poems describing few parts of my own life and ideas. We are trapped in a void of our own creation that hope can either darken or illuminate. At the end it is up to us *to be **Consumed** by the cold, dark void or be the **Light** which pierces through it like a like a hand reaching out its warmth to you.*

# Acknowledgements

To The Readers taking a chance at my first book.

# 1. Leh Hoffnarr

**Leh Hoffnarr, Leh Hoffnarr, Leh Hoffnarr.**
I sat there on a willow bench
as Leh Hoffnarr,
wearing a winter coat
On this velvety night.

A willow lad across me,
weeping in his mother's arms
as blood gushed down from his nose,
as he had hit the cold, hard circus floor.

I sat there as a desperate clown,
wanting to turn his frown upside down.
But I knew deep down,
How can a man with cold hands
make a soul feel the warmth he lacked.

A part of me who had known the warmth,
envious of the willow lad,
desired what he had.

But knew could never
as my hands grew colder and colder.

A cactus like me,
born in an oasis.
Now lies in a cold desert
of his own making.

Birds can't perch on me,
Insects can't crawl on me,
Water stays within me
but it makes me forget the warmth
I once felt.

As I got up, ready to leave.
Glancing back at the willow lad
knowing the warmth will never reach me,
and I'll never have what he had.

I walked into the velvety night,
hugging my coat tighter and tighter.
The stars grew fainter and fainter.
As a bridge appeared before me,
I walked to the edge
gazing upon the cold, dark , haunting waters.
The stars grew fainter and fainter by the second
and... *PLATSCH.*

*Tot Hoffnarr, Tot Hoffnarr, Tot Hoffnarr.*

**-by Amogh Jha**

# 2. Tot Hoffnarr

**Tot Hoffnarr, Tot Hoffnarr, Tot Hoffnarr.**
The cold, dark water called out to me
in a quiet lilt,
which I haven't heard since.

My cold hands started reaching out to it,
like a salmon thirsty for its untamed springs.

Without an insight I jumped towards it,
like the willow lad reaching into his mother's arms.

The distance grew closer and closer
and then...*PLATSCH*

The thrash enveloped my body.
As I looked beyond the surface
seeing the stars grow even fainter,
and my soul grew colder and colder.

Falling into the cold blue Abyss.

The cold embracing me,
like a mother embracing the body
of her lifeless child,
whom she'll never meet.

The cold needles piercing my heart,
still felt duller than the one's
I was embedded with.

Hope still lingered with me,
as I tried fleeing the Abyss.

The Abyss was frosting,
yet it felt warmer than the world I've been living in.

The hope in me,
attracted the darkness which engulfed me.
As I sank and sank to the bottom of the Abyss,
yet it felt brighter than the world I've been living in.

The glimmer of hope bloomed,
as it made me embrace the warm conclusion.

Knowing I will never feel this,
I stopped the struggle
and let it consume me.

As I sank and sank to the bottom of the Abyss,
The glowing void.
Hoffnarr, Hoffnarr, Hoffnarr.

**-by Amogh Jha**

# 3. Muse called Life

**Life the loudest Muse of all.**
You run through life,
unsure of where you'll be.
You write poetry
for every sight you see.

You bleed,
You cry,
You laugh,
You love,
You live.

It is a Muse which always talks to you.
I love and hate it
all at the same time,
But I know it is the best thing that will ever happen
in this lifetime.

The pain,
The love,

The beauty
is what makes it worth traveling.


Without time hope will cease to exist,
as we only hope thinking we have time.
And without Life time would cease
as you won't be there to experience it.


Life is fuelled by hope.
Hope to think someday everything will be good.
Hoping is cruel
but without hoping
a man can never push through.


**-by Amogh Jha**

# 4. A Version I Aspire

**What do I want to be?**
A better version of me
Or a dead living being.

I wanna be able to look back
and thank the past me for all he has done.
I wanna be able to look at future me
and assure him that I'll give him peace.

I will maintain the past self's hopes and dreams,
as he had done the same for me.

I will work towards being a kinder man,
A gentler man,
A stronger man.
A man who never loses hope,
never gives up,
never doubts that he has infinite possibilities.

Whenever he fails he gets back up.

He loves his valued ones.
He gives his all even if the conclusion is unsure.
He has a heart which is always so pure.
He laughs, he cries and
he faces everything with a smile.

He understands people,
He lives every moment,
He is a man who is at peace with himself.

Most important of all,
He doesn't hold back himself.
He fights with himself,
not letting him hold himself back

A man who has achieved his longing peace,
Not in heaven nor hell
but on this Erde.

This is a version
I Aspire to be.
But for now,
I'll stick with poetry.

**-by Amogh Jha**

# 5. Last Orchid on Earth

**Last Orchid on Earth.**
A flower of hope.
A flower of lust.

The Orchid sat in front of
The last man on earth,
like a mistress in court.

To the man she was a glimmer of life,
a glimmer of lustful hope.

It reassured the man,
that life will start to thrive
On this barren dead land.

The Orchid stood their
firmly yet delicately.
It was a sign,
That our Earth will restore.

The Last man was thirsty for hope and love.
The beauty was too much
for a thirsty man,
nearing his conclusion.

He knew he was wrong,
his temptation was wrong.
He knew he couldn't be with the beauty
he admired and loved.

He knew it was wrong to take the hope of the Earth
for his own selfish desires,
yet he got lost in the flower of love,
the flower of hope.

At last he plucked,
The Last Orchid on Earth.

In his hands the flower felt lost,
In his hands it couldn't live.
It lost its life and turned to bits.

The life of the man also concluded,
as the hope he had
left his hand.

At the end there wasn't a single beauty left

on this barren, hopeless rock.

**-by Amogh Jha**

# 6. Misunderstood Nights

**I misunderstood the nights.**
I thought that nights are scary,
a time when life doesn't exist.
A blanket of dead silence
covering the world.
A thick layer of mist.


Night,
The time when the otherworldly phantoms rise.


Little me thought that
"Nights are scary,
I will just sleep early,
So the otherworldly can't get me."


But now nights feel like it's embracing me.
A warm hug with a gift of peace.
A time for me to think.
A time when creating becomes easy.
Ideas bloom in my mind

and disperse the seeds.

Don't get me wrong,
Nights are still scary
but now I don't hate it,
as it brings me closer to inner me.

It's a time for the quiet to speak with themselves,
a time to be burned for their passion.
It's a time to reflect,
a time to create,
a time to be better,
and a time to be great.

The nights aren't so scary,
the quiet, the mist,
are all an opportunity
To be the one you aspire to be.
*To Carpe Noctem.*

**-by Amogh Jha**

# 7. O' to Love a Rock

**O' to Love a Rock.**
I once was a rock,
in a valley
submerged in mist.
It was dark,
and I couldn't see a thing.

One day a red rock appeared before me
out of thin air.
It shone brightly through the valley,
and suddenly the mist cleared
and sunlight hit my surface.

It felt nice but I shrugged it,
and went back to being a rock,
doing my own thing.
But there was a crack on my surface.

After a while,
the red rock started rolling downhill

far and away,
getting fainter and fainter.

That's when it hit me,
"Oh that rock sure is lovely."
And suddenly I broke,
into a million shards
of every imaginable color.
From the wreckage
I rose once more,
But this time,
as a dark red flower.

I looked towards the red rock,
admiring it's beauty.
Doing my best
to prevent it from fading.
But deep down I knew,
what it's like being a rock,
as I was once a rock
in this misty abyss,
until the red rock cracked my shell,
and made me into the dark red flower.

O' to love a rock is painful,
it's impossible to let it become a flower.
A rock can never become a flower

as I was the only exception.

I knew it was painful
but I let it be,
as I looked at the sky,
my petals turned to bits.

I wanted to hope but knew it is wrong,
as it had fooled a man named Hoffnarr.
But a drop stayed in me,
as I will be reborned,
not as a rock
but as a pebble of love.
The mist came back,
but it wasn't as thick as it was before.

**-by Amogh Jha**

# 8. As I Burned 1

**As I Burned,**
screaming for mercy,
screaming that I am innocent.
Praying to every God ever in existence.

I the mother of Willow,
soon to be mother of Orchid.
Being punished for crimes I never did,
by the devils who had done the same to ones before me.

They barged into my house like hungry wolves,
dragging me away from my child,
who can't survive a night without my warmth.

They dragged me, tried me
and locked me in a cold cell.
Called me a witch
and prepared for my end.

But I needed to be hopeful

for the Orchid in my womb.

She gave me strength
as I started scratching the cell.
I scratched and scratched and scratched
desperately for a life I had.
I scratched till all my nails tore off,
till my hands bathed in the blood,
till my throat hurt.

With those bloody hands
I embraced my Orchid,
But she wasn't their,
her warmth had disappeared
and so did my hope.

She had ascended
to a place unknown.

Tears swooped down,
as darkness surrounded me,
I sat in it,
felling empty,
until I saw a light.
My Willow
who was waiting for me.

As I reached out to embrace him,
I realized
I couldn't,
as I was tied to a pole
infront of the entire town.

**-by Amogh Jha**

# 9. As I Burned 2

*From the pole,*
I saw friends, relatives, neighbors
whom I had done everything for.
I thought I must be saved
as people I loved were there.

But as I took a hard look,
I saw a hatred, a disgust in their eyes
which I had never seen in my life.

I saw my lad,
weeping as always,
trying to run towards my soon to be grave
but was knocked out by those devils
who took even this hope away from me.

Soon It felt like the ground erupted.
It felt like I had stepped on molten lead.
Hell had been raised on me,
not by the Devil

but the people of this Erde.

I cried, I begged, I prayed.
I prayed to every God their was,
I asked the gods about what did I do wrong.

As I burned
and burned
and burned.
All the prayers seemed to be in vain,
as at the end
none of them came to my aid.
Not even the devil showed up to laugh
neither did the reaper to collect my heart.
As I found myself
in a Void made of hatred.

**-by Amogh Jha**

# 10. The Void

**What is the void ?**
You might ask.
An entity,
Another realm,
Hell,
Heaven
or even nothing at all.

Frankly I don't know it fully,
as the more you explore,
the more it grows.
But from what I know
I'll pass it on to you readers.

The Void is mysterious place,
with a soul of its own.
It's a place stretching beyond end.
A place which is filled with nothing but darkness.

A place which is worse than hell itself.

A place so quite
that you can hear your own despair.
A place which suffocates you for eternity.
A place where you are the only entity.

A place made up from despair,
from lack of hope,
and unknown to warmth.

Created when a person gives up,
when he had enough.
Created when a soul becomes hollow.
Created when their is nothing but sorrow.

It clouds the person's eyes
preventing it from seeing the beauty of life.

It is a place everyone fears to go.
A place which is filled with nothing.

It isn't that bad though.
The emptiness, the fear will make your heart grow.
It changes a man's outlook on life
cause nothing seems worse than the Void
but it also destroys one's life.

Some people stay in it till their demise.

They prefer the emptiness over the hope of a new life.
But the Void isn't a good place to be,
it's worse than anything there is.

But there is way out of it.
You have to be the hope that pierces through it.
You have to fill it with the warmth you had,
even though you might have cold hands.

The Void doesn't hate you,
as the door to exit is never closed.
It might just be infront of you
but you avoid it for a place with nothing.

The door to enter is also open,
it's up to you if you want to enter again,
Or you are made to
by the hope you cling onto.

The Void in you is nothing
compared to the great will you carry.
The heart in you which won't be shattered by any.

**-by Amogh Jha**

# 11. Light

*I used to dwell in the middle of the void.*
*Stabbing myself as time didn't exist.*
*Covering my eyes in a blanket of mist,*
*as I ceased to exists,*
*turning into bits.*

*Suddenly*
*A light pierced through the nothingness,*
*passing through the fog like a shining knight.*
*The void started disappearing*
*and the world regained its beauty.*
*Teeming with hope,*
*Teeming with life.*

*I looked beyond the light*
*to realize*
**Its source was I.**

**-by Amogh Jha**

# 12. My pointless poem at 13

The sun is shining so bright
But my days are like non luminous nights.

My dreams were broken in the era of despair.
The flame of life was flickering
till it disappeared.

Crying in the rains was more vivid,
than smiling at the bright sun.
The grudge in you won't let you express the true you.
People love the sun
but rains are more fun.

Happiness has an end
but sadness will come again.
All the misery holding me back from being who I am.

Life is just like scattered pieces of glass
that were once together
But they still show your reflection.

Even if the glass is delicate
remember it is made up of wise rocks.

*So this is how the recently turned teen me felt,*
*kinda pointless if I look from where I am.*
*He was stupid and everything was new,*
*yet he started something which lead to me writing*
*poetry.*
*The first one's aren't always that good*
*but still it sparked something new.*

**-by Amogh Jha**

# 13. Petrichor: the Joy in Rains

**Petrichor.**
The scent of God.
The smell of soil
after the first rain,
reminding that we will be liberated
from the oppression of heat.

Petrichor,
a fragrance which touches the soul.
The smell which is the language of the soil.

Petrichor,
reminding us that the rainy days have started,
but even in this turmoil
the smell of the soil
makes us understand the beauty of life.

It reassures,
gives us hope

that even in the heaviest of rains
there will be Petrichor.

**-by Amogh Jha**

# 14. Ehren Sucher

**Ehren Sucher, Ehren Sucher, Ehren Sucher.**
I the Ehren Sucher,
a man who romanticized war
but was unwissend of the horrors it caused.

I was a young lad,
in the era when a warrior was noblest of all.
Bloodshed was common
and men had the ego of a bubble,
can be popped with the slightest of touch.

We idealized war and blood.
Fought over the smallest things,
to protect our fake honor from others.
The honor which only we had control over.

Once an opportunity came my way,
to join the war,
and show my strength.
But if I had known

the hell that would be born.


Battle started, blood spilled,
heads flew,
and the applaud of bloodlust filled the theater of war.


I saw my comrades lose their soul,
I saw desperate men trying to cling onto hope.
Suddenly a man rushed towards me,
to defend I swinged my sword
but for some reason it felt heavier than ever.
In desperation I broke through the force
and next thing I knew,
his head was flying off.
The blood landed on my tongue
and now I was craving more.


As blood covered my eyes
and I went rouge.
Until I heard a cry
and the blood rolled out of my mind.
There I stood with a sword in the heart
of the man who had been my friend since I could walk.


The realization hit me,
disgust filled me,
and hatred bloomed in my heart,

hate for everything.

The pressure was too much for a lad like me,
as I fainted and was teleported to a realm of hatred.
After a while I woke up,
in a battlefield filled with despair.
Seemed like I was the only one alive.


**-by Amogh Jha**

# 15. Erloesung Sucher

I ran from that hell,
to find shelter,
to avoid the death by being caught.
Until I stepped and fell
onto the body of my first corpse.
In his pocket I saw a paper.
The paper with a painting of him and his whole world,
his wife and daughter.

Suddenly everything started turning black,
and I found myself in a place worse than hell.

Is being a warrior to hate yourself?
Is being a warrior to destroy families of men?
Is being a warrior to have a life without peace?
Is being a warrior to die in misery?

All these questions filled my mind
until a man's named shined
like a lonely star in the night sky.

A man who I had met once,
A man who was named Karlsefnie.
A man who was once out for bloody revenge
but now walks as a complete man.

How can a man with such bloodlust find peace ?
If he can do it then can me ?
Can a man like me be redeemed ?
Can a man like me pay for his sins ?

With a new found hope of paying for my sins,
I walked through the door
leaving the dark Abyss.

I woke up with bandages around me.
A woman who had found and cared for me.
I stayed with her till I recovered
but ended up falling in love.

After a while we had a child,
A man I believed was gonna be the star of my night.
My child,
the young Hoffnarr.


**-by Amogh Jha**

# 16. Scary dream I had

You know what is the most scary dream?
Knowing that you are in a dream is the scariest.
You might argue
that I can create anything in it
knowing it's a dream.
But dreams aren't a safe place.

I went to sleep af 12:30am that night.
My dream started as I was on a family trip.
We were staying at a place which we knew was haunted.
I went to sleep there and in bed realized,
that this might be a dream.

I shut my eyes tightly
forcing my mind
to get out of this dream.

Suddenly a holy song started playing,
then I heard my mother trying to wake me,
like she always does before school.

I woke up seeing my parents beside me,
filling a form for my sister's school trip or something.
I tried asking but in vain.
I had watched a video that day,
which told to never ask date and time in a dream,
Also you might wake up in another dream.


I tried looking at the clock
but it was blurry.
I opened my tablet beside me
and saw the date
it was 22nd February.
Which was weird as it was 8.
I was scared.


I tried waking up again,
This time I did wake up in the real world,
I pinched myself
and it hurt.
I looked at the clock
it was 1am.
I still couldn't believe it was real.


Them I fell asleep and woke up again,
this time in the morning
and wrote it then.

I got scared of sleeping for few days,
Who knows what if I was trapped in another dream
maize,
What if I get stuck there for days
but in the real world it'll just be a few minutes.


So dreams are one of my biggest fears,
as they are fun and weird,
They are scary and uncanny.
But I don't have a control over it.


**-by Amogh Jha**

# 17. A letter in my Old Journal

I found my old journal
while cleaning my drawer.
It had a letter which I wrote to myself.
Why not tell you readers about it
through a little poem.

*I know life is hard dear,*
*you overthink alot dear.*
*One day you think you messed up your friendship with*
*people*
*and one day you realize they don't hate you dear.*

*One day you blame others for the pain*
*but one day you realize it was all you dear.*

*Suffering is life dear.*
*Don't beat yourself up for little things dear.*
*Life is beautiful dear,*
*cherish it till the end dear.*

*Love yourself dear.*
*Give everything your all dear.*
*Sometimes peace and coffee is all you need dear.*

*I know you can't find your dream dear.*
*You don't know what to be dear*
*as you love little bit of everything dear.*
*Never back down if you are right dear.*
*There is no one you have to fight dear*
*not even yourself dear.*
*Just be better everyday dear.*

**You're in the middle of an ocean looking for any island**
**to harbor**
**But you cant find any**
**So you just wander aimlessly, feeling lost, uncertain of**
**what your path is**
**You just don't know what to do**
**You dont know which way to follow**
**So you just stay still, in the middle of nowhere**
**Being hollow.**

*At the end I just want to say,*
*Smile more often you corpse.*

**-by Amogh Jha**

# 18. My Little Percy

**My little Percy.**
I still remember the day you left me for heaven.
A day I'll remember forever.
The most griefious day of my existence till then.
You like a daughter, like a best friend.

You a tiny dog who got scared of cats.
Your left ear was cut in half,
your eyes full black,
filled with innocence.

You kinda reminded me of toothless.
I still remember seeing you as a tiny little stray.
To be honest I was a little afraid.
One day from heavens know where,
I got the courage to pet you and brush your hair.

Sometimes I think to myself,
If that day never happened atleast I won't be this sad,
But the thought of never knowing you in this life is bad.

After that day it wasn't the same,
you wagged your tail every time you saw my face.
We shared a joyful bond.
Whenever days were rough and I felt sad,
you'd always be there
and petting your head made it better than ever.

I taught you tricks like handshake,
for some reason you learned to roll on command.
You loved belly rubs and tickle on your cut ear.

I still remember how we raced and played tag.
You'd race me and win alot of times,
You'd chase me till I pet you.

You was obsessed with chicken,
every time I brought you it,
You'd snatch it right out of my hand.

The evenings when you lied on my lap,
you'd follow me to my home.
I'd throw you treats out the window and you would
catch.

Just when I was preparing to officially adopt you,
You had to leave this body

and transcend to the heavens.

You'd always wait for me to play.
My biggest regret is not having a moment to say
goodbye to you,
You left me without a word
for God's abode.
And I will miss you till I conclude and join you.


**-by Amogh Jha**

# 19. A Thousand Bridges

**I stand on side of a valley.**
A valley with a thousand bridges.
Some broken, some safe,
Some nonexistent and some just plain.

Some bridges are being built for me,
and some I have to build.
I am being suggested to choose the safest bridge.

The safest bridge is good I must say,
but it is really boring and stale.
I know I might have the speed to run through it quickly
and reach the other side faster than any.

But I wanna walk the bridge of my own making.
The other bridges are noble I must say,
But I wanna walk alot of them,
but once I reach the other side
there is no going back.

So I'll just use small pieces of every bridge,
to make one
even though I am not good at it.

Maybe it'll be weak,
Maybe it'll break
and I will fall into the valley of despair.

But it is still better than walking the ones
built by others.

I tried making the bridge
but was stopped by the builders
as they knew I didn't had the power to.
They said you just doing this for fun,
if you were determined
then you should have been an early bird.

I really wanted to build that bridge.
But was stopped by my own foolish.

I think to myself,
what if I took parts from every bridge
and changed the safest
to my liking.

I am still confused what bridge to travel by,

and if it takes more time
then I will miss the sunset.

Should I just stop traveling,
or should I travel every.
But I know it is not possible,
so here I am sitting
and doing poetry.

**-by Amogh Jha**

# 20. The Willow Lad

**I The Willow Lad.**

I the son of the witch,
and murderer of my father.

I the man who killed his lover.
I the man who avoided love.
I the man who burned my own people.

I the man who was blinded by revenge.
I the man who did everything to never feel warm again.
The warmth is scary
as it leads to misery.

I the man who denied every god.
I the man who wanted to kill them all.
I the man who is friends with the void.
I the man who now thinks destroyed his life.

The realization occurred
when I saw a child with his dead mother.

Who had been slayed by my hands.
I saw the hate
I saw him staring into my Void.
That's when I understand
that all I did to avoid the warmth
will lead to my cold demise.

I saw the boy pick up a knife.
I gave up and he plucked my eyes.
He stabbed me with a voided face.

I felt life fleeing myself.
At the end all I saw was his eyes.
The eyes of a person
who'll be the first step
of the end of this Erde.

**-by Amogh Jha**

# 21. Brightest Cruel of Life

**What is Hope?**
As I asked myself this question,
sitting in a void of my own creation.

A part of me whispered,
"It is the fuel which lights our existence.
It gives us purpose,
It gives us strength,
It stands with us
when nobody does.
It's a barrier preventing us
from entering the spiral of despair.
It fuels us to never give up."

Another part of me hissed.
Expressing dissent he murmured,
"It is a promise for a future
which is a fiction.
It is a lie to our soul
to keep it going,

But at the end
when realization occurs,
that what we hope will never happen to us.
Therefore breaking the soul into a million fragments."

As the smoke of burning hope,
Spirals around us.
It gives birth to the void inside us.

Hope is the ray of light,
piercing through the void like a shining knight.

Hope is also the darkness,
strengthening the walls of our castle.

As both were done with their opening statement,
I sat there as a judge deciding the final verdict.
They both had left me speechless,
yet at the end I still wanted to be hopeful,
as without hope no one can live in this world.
Hope is something we give ourself,
It stays with us until the end.
It fools us like Leh Hoffnarr,
yet it is what makes us push through
the darkest of voids.

Hope is a beautiful and the brightest
Cruel of Life.

**-by Amogh Jha**